Morris County
MEMORIES
THE EARLY YEARS ~ 1850-1939

ACKNOWLEDGMENTS

The *Daily Record* is pleased to present *"Morris County Memories."* It must be noted, however, that this unique pictorial book would not have been possible without the generous contributions made by many people and organizations from virtually every corner of our county.

We are indebted, first of all, to those early Morris County residents who captured their times – our history – in photographs, and provided us with a glimpse into their lives.

Secondly, all Morris County residents are indebted to the many individuals who are committed to preserving our history in various libraries, historical societies, museums, archives and personal collections throughout the county.

The following organizations have contributed greatly to
"Morris County Memories: The Early Years ~ 1850 - 1939"

Boonton Historical Society and Museum

Denville Historical Society and Museum

Historical Society of the Township of Chatham

Lake Hopatcong Historical Society

Madison Historical Society

Madison Public Library

Morris County Historical Society

Morris Plains Museum

Morristown/Morris Township Free Public Library

Parsippany Historical and Preservation Society

Picatinny Arsenal

Whippany Railway Museum

Copyright© 2001 • ISBN: 1-891395-71-8

Published by Pediment Publishing, a division of The Pediment Group, Inc. www.pediment.com printed in Canada

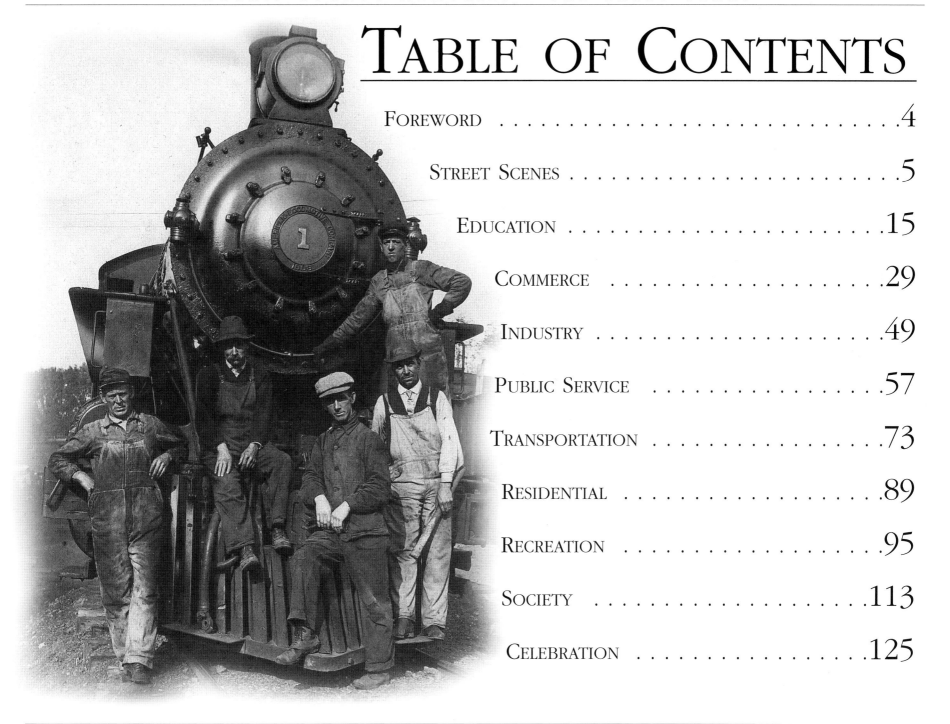

TABLE OF CONTENTS

FOREWORD

We are very happy to bring you these memories of the early years of Morris County.

They're not the earliest: We were already well-dug in here in the awful winter of 1779-1780 when George Washington quartered his Revolutionary War troops outside Morristown. But they do give us an often-forgotten picture of how we were more than 100 years later, just before and after 1900, when the streets in Morristown (crowded and thriving even then) were dirt, young ladies at Miss Dana's School wore floor-length dresses and soldiers carrying rifles embarked from Dover for the Spanish American War.

Coincidentally, it was during the same time (1900) that the first *Daily Record* was printed in Morristown. Price? Two cents. Circulation? A couple thousand.

These pictures don't presume to record the important moments of history. They merely give us a slice of life, often everyday life, around the turn of the century.

For more than 100 years, the *Daily Record* has been a part of the lives of the people who live and work in Morris County. We're proud that our newspaper is a part of your life, whether it's unfolding at your breakfast table, billowing in the breeze on your front porch in the summer, shared with loved ones before a crackling fire in the winter or tucked securely under an arm on the way to the office.

The *Daily Record* is Morris County's newspaper and we provide the most Morris County news to our readers every day. Like most newspapers, we see ourselves as the first step in recording history. Long before the books are published, before news hits the glossy pages of a magazine, newspapers chronicle events every day. Our pages include the events that matter to people's lives – from birth announcements to high school graduations, from sports achievements to professional milestones, from wedding announcements to obituaries, Morris County residents see their lives and their neighbors' lives unfold in our pages.

A hundred years after our birth, Morris County has changed, and we've changed, too. Our technology has changed from letter-by-letter typesetting, past the first generation printing press to today's offset printing with high quality color photographs and advertising. But, some things remain the same: Our commitment to our local community … to friendly customer service … to accuracy and honesty.

We are pleased to bring you this book of the early memories of Morris County in addition to bringing the most Morris County news to your home every day.

Walt Lafferty
President & Publisher

STREET SCENES

We've all seen old cars in the movies. In the pages that follow you'll see them as they really appeared in Morris County — quaint and somehow comic from our perch in the 21st century. You also see their predecessors, the horse and buggy, as foreign to us as the first cars and looking strangely out of place along the city streets of Morristown.

You may not have expected those streets to be dirt. Even the busiest ones were unpaved, from the blocks around the Morris County Courthouse to main streets in Denville, Wharton and Mendham. Dirt made sense given that most of the horse-power then came from the real thing.

Not long thereafter came the trolley cars and the power lines above them, as well as the traffic control booth on Park Place in Morristown. Of course, by today's standards, cars still appeared few and far between.

The nearby Green looked as beautiful then as it does today. In Madison, mean-while, the trains still ran at street level. Gates stopped road traffic at the appropri-ate moments.

These were days were people still dried their laundry outside and kids pulled carts with stagecoach-like, iron-rimmed wheels.

Waverly Place looking from Kings Road to Main Street prior to the elevation of the railroad tracks, Madison, 1913.
Courtesy of Madison Public Library

Main Street, Madison, 1906. *Courtesy of Madison Public Library*

Green Village Road, looking north across Kings Road, Madison, circa 1913. *Courtesy of Madison Public Library*

Green Avenue looking south to Chatham Township prior to elevation of railroad, Madison, 1913. *Courtesy of Madison Public Library*

Kings Road looking toward Morristown from the corner of Prospect Street. St. Vincent's and Green Avenue School are visible in the background, Madison, 1913. *Courtesy of Madison Public Library*

Bank Street, Morristown, 1910. *Courtesy of Morristown/Morris Township Free Public Library*

Main Street, New Vernon, circa 1905. *Courtesy of Historical Society of the Township of Chatham*

View looking from Central Avenue to Waverly Place. Note the man on the flag-pole, Madison, circa 1917. *Courtesy of Madison Public Library*

The business section of Morris Plains, 1920. Businesses in this stretch included an expanded Merchant's store, Morris Plains Bakery, Morris Plains Shoe Repair, Zecca's Ice Cream, Elzerman's Restaurant and others. The post office is to the right. *Courtesy of Morris Plains Museum*

Keep Street, Madison, looking west, November 6, 1913. *Courtesy of Madison Public Library*

A view of Mt. Pleasant Avenue in Whippany looking toward the eastern section of Hanover (present-day East Hanover) and beyond that, Livingston, circa 1880. Today, this view would be the eastbound side of Route 10 near the intersection with Troy Hills Road. The small building in the foreground was the Polhemus Emporium. It was later moved and became part of the much larger Polhemus Hall, which survives today, in slightly altered form on Route 10 East. *Courtesy Steve Hepler collection*

Court Street looking from Ann Street toward Washington Street, Morristown, early 1900s. *Courtesy of Morristown/Morris Township Free Public Library*

Panoramic view of the Morristown Green – looking north. *Courtesy of Morristown/Morris Township Free Public Library*

Panoramic view of the Morristown Green – looking east. *Courtesy of Morristown/Morris Township Free Public Library*

Traffic control booth on Park Place, Morristown. *Courtesy of Morristown/Morris Township Free Public Library*

A view of Main Street, Denville, looking toward Bloomfield Avenue, circa 1915. The Wayside Inn is on the left. *Courtesy of Denville Historical Society and Museum*

Looking southeast down Main Street (Route 53) past Bloomfield Avenue, Denville, circa 1939. *Courtesy of Denville Historical Society and Museum*

A view of Speedwell Avenue, Morristown, 1918. *Courtesy of Morristown/Morris Township Free Public Library*

A view of Main Street, Wharton, late 1800s. *Courtesy of Morris County Historical Society*

West Main Street, Mendham, circa 1906. *Courtesy of Morris County Historical Society*

Dover decorated for the Old Home Week parade held in August of 1910. *Courtesy of Lake Hopatcong Historical Society*

Route 53 in Mount Tabor, looking north, circa 1910. This is the Simpson Avenue entrance to Mount Tabor. *Courtesy of Parsippany Historical and Preservation Society*

A view of Myrtle Avenue and Main Street, Boonton, circa 1928. *Courtesy of Boonton Historical Society and Museum*

Main Street, Boonton, early 1900s. *Courtesy of Boonton Historical Society and Museum*

Sussex Street, Dover, looking south from Clinton Street, 1910. The decorations are for Old Home Week, celebrated in August of 1910. *Courtesy of Morris County Historical Society*

EDUCATION

How different the schools were! And how different we looked!

Although some students dressed in everyday wear, others decked out in far more formal attire of the late 19th and early 20th centuries. In 1886 in Madison, for instance, the young ladies in Miss Lovell's class wore fashionable, high-necked, button-up dresses and leg o' mutton sleeve blouses, and broad-brimmed hats big enough for flowers. The wealthy women at Miss Dana's School on South Street in Morristown were older and even dressier, with long, flowing skirts and layers upon layers of coats and shawls and shirts, puffed up sleeves and hair showing obvious signs of importance. Not a piece of skin below the neck is visible. In contrast, kids at an outing for the Morris County Children's Home looked downright threadbare.

There were one-room schoolhouses, two-room schoolhouses and schools housed in what looked like big, expensive private homes. The Green Avenue School in Madison looked like a church, as did Brookside's.

What these pictures show most clearly is the drastic difference in population.

The recording of Boonton High School's class of 1900 shows 10 girls in beautiful white lace dresses and two boys in dark three-piece suits. (Boonton's class of 2001 had more than 100 graduates.) Morristown High School's diploma-carrying, flower-festooned class of 1909 consisted of 15 deadly earnest girls carrying more lace and flowers than you would see anywhere outside a wedding, and seven boys in equally resplendent ties and collars. (Morristown's class of 2001 had more than 300 students.)

Miss Dana's School on South Street, Morristown, circa 1900. *Courtesy of Morristown/Morris Township Free Public Library*

Morristown Select Classical School, at the home of Henry O. Pitney, June 1872. Those identified: Sarah Louisa Pitney, Vernon Murray Bokee, Henry O. Pitney, Olin B. Coit, John O.H. Pitney, George L. Wright, Wilbert Warren Perry, Theo. Ayers Jr., John B. Ayers, Walter B. Wood, Sadie H. Pitney, H.O. Pitney Jr., James A. Webb Jr., Katherine J. Pitney, Mary Brayton Pitney, F.W. Merrell, Alfred Elmer Mills, Meyer L. Sire, Chas. H. Davis, Benjamin Sire, D. Hunter McAlpin Jr., H.K. Toler, Albert I. Sire, R. McAlpin, Wm. W. McAlpin Ingersoll, Olmsted L. Baker, William Meeker Wood, George L. Cobb, Addison H. Hazeltine, Alfred E. Decamp, Mahlon Pitney, Edward A. Auir, Paul Revere, Nathan Bozeman, Augustus W. Bell Jr., George L. McAlpin, Harry B. McCarroll, Edward L. Hopkins, Thomas M.F. Randolph. *Courtesy of Morristown/Morris Township Free Public Library*

Women peer in the windows of Denville's second Union School, built in 1861. *Courtesy of Denville Historical Society and Museum*

Classroom at Miss Hazeltine's Private School, Morristown, late 1800s. *Courtesy of Morristown/Morris Township Free Public Library*

Class of 1889 with teacher, Mr. Johnson, in front of the Denville School, No. 11, built in 1855, that stood next to the Community Church on Diamond Spring Road. *Courtesy of Denville Historical Society and Museum*

Miss Lovell's class, Madison, circa 1886. *Courtesy of Madison Historical Society*

Students from Miss Dana's School, Morristown, early 1890s. *Courtesy of Morristown/Morris Township Free Public Library*

Dedication of Green Avenue School, Madison, circa 1879. *Courtesy of Madison Historical Society*

Students on the steps of Green Avenue School, September 28, 1891. *Courtesy of Madison Public Library*

Madison Academy, circa 1895. *Courtesy of Madison Historical Society*

Students in front of the Denville two-room schoolhouse, built in 1894. Photo, circa 1912. *Courtesy of Denville Historical Society and Museum*

Grade school students in an unidentified classroom. From left, Haskell Hewson, Lois Whitaker, Robert Sniffen, Irving Williams, Catherine McGraw, Dorothy Hedden, Marcia Schenck, Smith Taylor, Roger Lum, Robert McKinney, unidentified, Leonora Conklin and Harriet Rathbun, circa 1906. *Courtesy of Madison Historical Society*

Boonton High School graduating class of 1900. *Courtesy of Boonton Historical Society and Museum*

Brookside public school, Mendham, circa 1907. *Courtesy of Morristown/Morris Township Free Public Library*

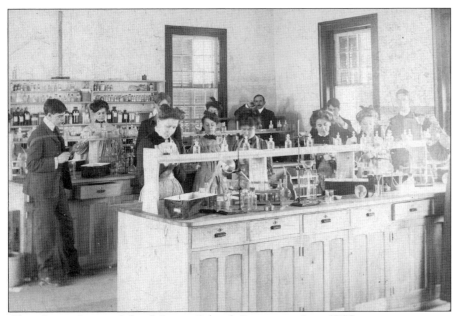

Chemistry class at School Street School, Boonton, circa 1902. *Courtesy of Boonton Historical Society and Museum*

Classroom at Miss Dana's School, Morristown, circa 1900. *Courtesy of Morristown/Morris Township Free Public Library*

Mendham schoolhouse, circa 1900. *Courtesy of Morristown/Morris Township Free Public Library*

Red Brick School, Chatham Township, circa 1907. *Courtesy of Historical Society of the Township of Chatham*

Morristown High School class of 1909. *Courtesy of Morris County Historical Society*

St. John's School on Cornelia Street, Boonton, circa 1912. *Courtesy of Boonton Historical Society and Museum*

The private school at the Smith House, June 1916. From left, front row, Arthur Paulniere Jr., Jack Crowell and Elizabeth Mitchell. Middle row, Florence Condit, Fred Crowell Jr., Irene Kitchell, Horace Paulniere and Adelaide Baldwin. Back row, Frances Cobb, Emily Baldwin, Florence Howell Prish (teacher), Margaret Brown and Katherine Mitchell. *Courtesy of Parsippany Historical and Preservation Society*

Students and faculty pose in front of their new schoolhouse on West Hanover Avenue, Morris Plains, 1908. Andrew Coffey and his dog, Buster, can be seen in front row center. *Courtesy of Morris Plains Museum*

Students of Center Grove School House, Randolph, circa 1906. *Courtesy of Morris County Historical Society*

Graduating class of 1910, Middletown High School, Rockaway Township. Included in the photo are: Elsie Wells, Edith Tiger, Gladys Richards, Ashen Trenberth, Evelyn Moody, Jane Bockoren, Clara Brown, Mr. Many Dempsey, Jessie Sanson, Edna Oliver, Beatrice Lippman, Helen Price, Mable Lonards, Ethel Miller, Russell Pierson, Norman Tomlinson, Zella Strugis, Martha Daley, Amy Nebon, George Montieth, Walter Alexander, Elsie King, Dan Jensen, Genevieve Dunn, Herman Cone, Helen Ambrose and Harold Price. *Courtesy of Morristown/Morris Township Free Public Library*

Green Village School, Chatham Township, circa 1910. *Courtesy of Historical Society of the Township of Chatham*

Alpha Nu sorority, Morristown High School, circa 1910. Standing, Mary P. Dempsey, Jessie Samsons, Margaret O'Brien and Agnes Leonard. Middle row, Edith Trimmins, Helen Muir, Luella Stephen, Ada Eccles and Gertrude Wise. Front row, Alice Prost, Mary Pierson and Lillian Ball. *Courtesy of Morris County Historical Society*

Entire Boonton High School faculty, circa 1915. *Courtesy of Boonton Historical Society and Museum*

Boonton's School Street School 8th grade graduating class, 1917. *Courtesy of Boonton Historical Society and Museum*

Transportation stagecoach bringing children from Washington Valley and other areas to Hillside School, Morristown, circa 1914. *Courtesy of Morristown/Morris Township Free Public Library*

Boonton High School class, 1922. *Courtesy of Boonton Historical Society and Museum*

Members of Morris Plains High School class of 1918 in front of the library. *Courtesy of Morris Plains Museum*

An outing for the children of the Morris County Children's Home, Parsippany, 1926. *Courtesy of Parsippany Historical and Preservation Society*

St. Elizabeth College Convent, Florham Park. *Courtesy of Morristown/Morris Township Free Public Library*

Morris Plains Grammar School class of 1926. The school was attended by Parsippany public school pupils. Included in the photo are: William Decker, Jean Huber, Charles Burch, Marjorie Evans, Cip Lyon, Clara Wiedman, Don Kitchell, Muriel Rennie, Mildred Walton, Mr. Holcombe, Edna Mary Bardet, Henrietta Satoff, Anna Bladt, Louise Mount, Claris Camphle, Helen Mazzalo, Dorothy Willigus, Rose Chesney, Miss Ayres, Judson Davies, Edward Crayon, Alben Rheinhart, Henry Bardet, Edgar Thurston and George Van Winkle. *Courtesy of Parsippany Historical and Preservation Society*

First Morris Plains school on Hanover Avenue. *Courtesy of Morristown/Morris Township Free Public Library*

Pupils from the Collinsville School, Morristown, circa 1920. *Courtesy of Morristown/Morris Township Free Public Library*

Madison House, women's dormitory, Drew University. *Courtesy of Madison Public Library*

Jack Kitchell and the earliest Parsippany school bus, circa 1930. *Courtesy of Parsippany Historical and Preservation Society*

Miss Higeman's fifth through eighth grade class at Red Brick School, Chatham Township, 1928. *Courtesy of Historical Society of the Township of Chatham*

COMMERCE

In many respects, business was simpler back then — and harder.

Those were the days when the butcher used a horse and wagon to deliver to your home. Morristown had the most possibilities, of course. In close proximity you could find an ice house (even in summer), stationery and confectionery stores, fish market and gunsmith. You could buy groceries and clothes, send a telegram and get your horse shod.

If you were male (it seems) you could belly up to a bar. The place that sold newspapers also sold bicycles and Kodaks. If you got home delivery, the delivery boy wore a tie.

Morristown wasn't the only place of commerce, of course. Proprietors of the Baker Theater in Dover produced live entertainment before packed houses. The 1887 construction of the sumptuous Hotel Breslin, which had more than 300 rooms and displayed the wealth produced by the area's once-great iron industry, set the stage for the growth elsewhere of Lake Hopatcong as a hot-weather resort.

At Lee's Pavilion, a booming complex of hotel, restaurant and stores, you could see a movie for 10 cents.

President Grover Cleveland a few years earlier practiced a far slower recreation, rocking on the porch at a far smaller inn, the Denville House. Men got their hair cut in Boonton, bought real estate in Madison (known as the "Rose City" for the nearly 100 growers growing them) and enjoyed ice cream in Landing.

There were no chain stores then — just proud merchants in white aprons posing beneath stores that offered (usually) just what people needed.

The "Store at the Corner," Morris Plains, 1915. This building, at the southwest corner of Jaqui Avenue, housed a business as early as the mid-1700s when it was Jacob Young's provisions store. A century later, Isaac Clark was storekeeper. In 1887, Clark sold the business to one of his clerks, Dan Merchant. The small store would become the cornerstone of Merchant's many mercantile enterprises. At the time of this photo, Merchant was leasing the store to Hendrik Elzerman, who had a restaurant and ice cream parlor there. The building also served as a trolley station. *Courtesy of Morris Plains Museum*

W.F. Day Restaurant in Morristown. Included in the photo are: Edward Stanborough, Wiliam Roy, Fred Baldwin, William F. Day, Jean Mack, Jeanette Mack, Georgie Kinsey, Maynard Day, Gus, a French chef, Charles Williams, Samuel James, Fred Day, Harry Day, Charles Pfeiffer, Fred Kionis, John Day and Mrs. Day. W.F. Day rode the bicycle to Washington in two days, circa 1890. *Courtesy of Morristown/Morris Township Free Public Library*

John Van Dorn (left) and Lewis E. Applegit in front of the New York Cash Store, Morristown, circa 1890. The store sold linens, oriental rugs, hassocks, material, clothing and other items. *Courtesy of Morristown/Morris Township Free Public Library*

H.G. Emmell stationery store, Morristown, circa 1877. *Courtesy of Morristown/Morris Township Free Public Library*

J.W. Thompson store, G.W. Greene sewing machine store and H.G. Emmell stationery store, Morristown, circa 1890. *Courtesy of Morristown/Morris Township Free Public Library*

Adams & Fairchild store. From left to right: George C. Smith, Ammerman, William Sowers, Hudson H. Fairchild, Adams, Wolf, Nicholas B. Briant, James Sylvester Adams, Frank H. Fairchild and Edward A. Van Fleet, Morristown, circa 1886. *Courtesy of Morristown/Morris Township Free Public Library*

Interior of A.W. Theiler's Bar at 55 Speedwell Avenue, Morristown, circa 1890. *Courtesy of Morristown/Morris Township Free Public Library*

George Green & Sons leather goods and harness maker, Washington Street, Morristown, circa 1890. *Courtesy of Morristown/Morris Township Free Public Library*

Interior of Wise Bakery on Washington Street, Morristown, circa 1895. *Courtesy of Morristown/Morris Township Free Public Library*

Interior of H.G. Emmell stationery store. Mr. Emmell is wearing the cap, Morristown, circa 1890. *Courtesy of Morristown/Morris Township Free Public Library*

Morris Aqueduct Co. at 21 South Street. Frederic V. Pitney and Philander B. Pierson are seated at the desks, Morristown, circa 1895. *Courtesy of Morristown/Morris Township Free Public Library*

Willis H. Dutton machinist, Morristown, circa 1985. *Courtesy of Morristown/Morris Township Free Public Library*

B.C. Meeker (with bicycle) and Ed Nubu in front of Meeker's locksmith store, Morristown, circa 1890. *Courtesy of Morristown/Morris Township Free Public Library*

Gun smithing and general jobbing business, Morristown, circa 1890. *Courtesy of Morristown/Morris Township Free Public Library*

Adams & Fairchild grocers and Arnold and P.H. Hoffman & Son storefronts, Morristown, circa 1890. *Courtesy of Morristown/Morris Township Free Public Library*

Horse and buggy in front of the Wayside Inn, Denville, circa 1890. *Courtesy of Denville Historical Society and Museum*

H.G. Emmell stationery and book store, Morristown, circa 1890. *Courtesy of Morristown/Morris Township Free Public Library*

J.K. Boniface produce and fish market was the first store on South Street, Morristown, circa 1890. *Courtesy of Morristown/Morris Township Free Public Library*

United States Hotel in Boonton, late 1800s. The hotel was built in 1858. *Courtesy of Boonton Historical Society and Museum*

Shelley's Ice House, Center Street, Morristown, circa 1890. *Courtesy of Morristown/Morris Township Free Public Library*

Adams & Fairchild in Morristown, circa 1886. *Courtesy of Morristown/Morris Township Free Public Library*

The Denville Hotel, at the corner of Main Street and Bloomfield Avenue, October 1890. Seated third from the left (with top hat) on the porch is President Grover Cleveland, who visited Denville between his two non-consecutive terms as president (1885-1889 and 1893-1897). *Courtesy of Denville Historical Society and Museum*

M. Mulcahy Blacksmith Shop on Park Avenue, Madison, circa 1900. *Courtesy of Madison Historical Society*

Arlington Hotel, Mount Tabor, circa 1900. *Courtesy of Parsippany Historical and Preservation Society*

The grand and luxurious Hotel Breslin, built in 1887, set the stage for Lake Hopatcong's development as a resort. In 1918 it was renamed the Alamac Hotel. Seen in this 1910 photo, it was the largest hotel on Lake Hopatcong, containing some 300 rooms. *Courtesy of Lake Hopatcong Historical Society*

Production room of the Boonton Times, circa 1900. *Courtesy of Boonton Historical Society and Museum*

Central Market at 416 Main Street, Boonton, with its delivery wagon, circa 1900. *Courtesy of Boonton Historical Society and Museum*

Frank Giordano Sr. is driving the Giordano Bros. delivery truck, William Bell is in the window and Joseph is holding Spot the dog, Morristown, circa 1914. *Courtesy of Morristown/Morris Township Free Public Library*

William K. Muchmore (left) in front of his business on Speedwell Avenue, Morristown. *Courtesy of Morristown/Morris Township Free Public Library*

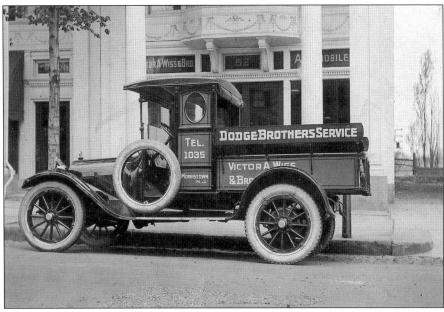

Delivery wagon of the Victor A. Wiss garage on South Street, Morristown. *Courtesy of Morristown/Morris Township Free Public Library*

Heinrich Elzerman stands behind the counter of his Confectionery and Ice Cream Parlor, Morris Plains, 1917. *Courtesy of Morris Plains Museum*

In the early years, when roads around Lake Hopatcong were poor or non-existent, most commerce was by water. For lakefront homeowners, dockside deliveries were common. However, items still needed to be brought to the lake, and large deliveries were necessary for the hotels. In this circa 1908 photograph, a delivery arrives from M.H. Fancher, a butcher in Kenvil. *Courtesy of Lake Hopatcong Historical Society*

Lee's Pavilion at Lake Hopatcong included a hotel with 30 rooms and a popular restaurant, seen in this circa 1910 photograph. The pavilion was destroyed by fire in 1924. *Courtesy of Lake Hopatcong Historical Society*

The Lake Hopatcong Yacht Club was founded in 1905 and broke ground for its clubhouse on Bertrand Island in 1909. This photograph was taken at its dedication on July 10, 1910. The club still uses the building, which has changed little since its construction. *Courtesy of Lake Hopatcong Historical Society*

Dover telegraph office, circa 1896. *Courtesy of Lake Hopatcong Historical Society*

As railroads spurred tourism, hotels were quickly built to accommodate visitors. In 1883, only four small hotels existed at Lake Hopatcong. By 1900, more than forty hotels and rooming houses were operating along the booming shores of the lake. One of Lake Hopatcong's earliest hotels was the Lake View in Mount Arlington. Dating from the 1870s, it grew to around 100 rooms, as seen in this circa 1910 photograph. *Courtesy of Lake Hopatcong Historical Society*

Denville Garage on Main Street in the 1920s. *Courtesy of Denville Historical Society and Museum*

Early stores at Lake Hopatcong were often bare bones. Flowers Store, seen in this circa 1908 photograph, operated in Landing on today's Lakeside Boulevard. *Courtesy of Lake Hopatcong Historical Society*

Built in 1906 and rebuilt for motion pictures in 1924, the Baker Theatre in Dover was the finest theatre in the area. It featured live entertainment in the early years. This photograph was taken in 1908. *Courtesy of Lake Hopatcong Historical Society*

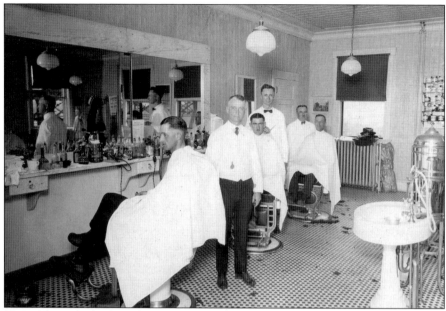

T. C. Edmonds' barber shop at 221 Main Street, Boonton, circa 1922. *Courtesy of Boonton Historical Society and Museum*

Upon arriving by train, visitors to Lake Hopatcong needed things to do, and two pavilions were built at Nolans Point. The first was the Nolans Point Pavilion. It later became known by the owner's name – Allen's Pavilion. It featured hotel rooms, stores, dancing, swimming, boat rentals and amusements. A Central Railroad of New Jersey train is visible in this 1910 photograph. *Courtesy of Lake Hopatcong Historical Society*

Pardee & Clark store on Blackwell Street in Dover, circa 1900. *Courtesy of Lake Hopatcong Historical Society*

Tourism began to boom at Lake Hopatcong when the Central Railroad of New Jersey reached Nolans Point in the early 1880s. This led to the building of two pavilions and several hotels at Nolans Point. In this circa 1910 photo, we see Lee's Pavilion, which included a hotel, restaurant, dance hall, stores, photo studio and Lake Hopatcong's first movie theater. Today, the Jefferson House Restaurant occupies a portion of this site. *Courtesy of Lake Hopatcong Historical Society*

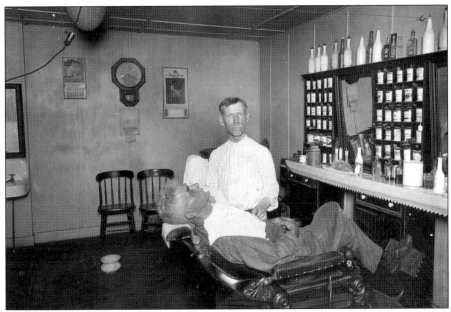

James Trimble in his barber shop in Boonton. In the chair is John Oliver. *Courtesy of Boonton Historical Society and Museum*

Exterior of the C. Benjamin Real Estate office. This was previously Larison's Drug Store on the southeast side of Waverly Place, Madison. Photo circa 1920. *Courtesy of Madison Public Library*

Andy Lusardi stands behind the marble counter in his confectionery store, Madison, circa 1934. *Courtesy of Madison Public Library*

One of the original grocery stores in Lake Hiawatha, circa 1930. *Courtesy of Parsippany Historical and Preservation Society*

Newspaper delivery crew in Morristown, circa 1920. *Courtesy of Morristown/Morris Township Free Public Library*

Barnee Google's along Route 46, Rockaway, circa 1930. Rockaway Sales, a hardware store, later occupied the same site. *Courtesy of Denville Historical Society and Museum*

Interior of Giordano Bros. Store, a grocery and butcher, owned by Frank Giordano, Morristown, 1937. *Courtesy of Morristown/Morris Township Free Public Library*

United States Hotel in Morristown, circa 1930. *Courtesy of Morristown/Morris Township Free Public Library*

Brookside Post Office and store, circa 1939. *Courtesy of Morristown/Morris Township Free Public Library*

The Palace Theatre opened in Netcong in 1919 and played a major role in borough life until its closing in 1980. It is now enjoying a second life as the home of the Growing Stage, a family oriented theater company. *Courtesy of Lake Hopatcong Historical Society*

Estler's Plumbing showroom on Main Street, Boonton, circa 1930. *Courtesy of Boonton Historical Society and Museum*

Dr. Arbuckle and Robert T. Lucas in the grocery store at the corner of Main and Plane streets in Boonton, circa 1933. *Courtesy of Boonton Historical Society and Museum*

Businesses in the Plaza Building, Morristown, circa 1935. *Courtesy of Morristown/Morris Township Free Public Library*

INDUSTRY

Ice wasn't made in the refrigerator. In fact, there were no refrigerators. Ice was harvested in the winter from Lake Hopatcong, kept frozen for months in straw and sawdust and then sold to ice companies throughout the state. Homeowners used the ice to keep their milk and meat cold in iceboxes even in the summer. It was backbreaking, cold-weather work for both men and horses, and it didn't die until the 1930s. Those iceboxes are now prized by antique lovers and can be found in living rooms holding plants and yarn.

Morris County was the place where iron ore was mined and turned into cannon balls for George Washington's Continental Army. Washington counted "80 to 100 iron-works, great and small" in the area, and by 1880 Morris County ranked third in the nation in production of iron ore. Some of those mines are still troubling homeowners today in towns like Mine Hill. Remains of some of the furnaces can be found in the woods, victims of far cheaper ore discovered near Lake Superior.

You can also find preserved remnants of the Morris Canal, where, beginning in the 1830s, horses pulled barges the 102 miles between the Hudson and Delaware rivers, bringing Morris County the Pennsylvania coal it so badly needed to make iron. In its day, it was a great advance in transportation, and ore production skyrocketed … for a while.

Ice harvesting at Lake Hopatcong. During the winter, blocks of ice would be shipped to Newark and New York by train or wagon. *Courtesy of Parsippany Historical and Preservation Society*

Ice harvesting on Lake Hopatcong, circa 1915. *Courtesy of Lake Hopatcong Historical Society*

From the mid 1800s to the 1930s, ice was a huge industry on Lake Hopatcong. At its peak, the lake supported five major ice houses, employing hundreds of laborers during the ice cutting season. Horses were widely used as they were considered more dependable than the machinery then available. Photo circa 1905. *Courtesy of Lake Hopatcong Historical Society*

This building stood on the site of the old forge at Old Boonton, where supplies were made for the Continental Army. It was here where iron from the adjacent mountains, carried on the backs of horses, was smelted and forged. *Courtesy of Morristown/Morris Township Free Public Library*

Camusat Bros. flower fields, Madison. *Courtesy of Madison Public Library*

Amedeo Micone on the step of the greenhouse with a bouquet of flowers, Madison, circa 1900. *Courtesy of Madison Public Library*

James M. Littlejohn, a native of Strathearn, Scotland, was hired by Judge Francis S. Lathrop of Madison in 1865 to supervise his greenhouse. He was considered a pioneer in rose growing. *Courtesy of Madison Public Library*

Noe Farm greenhouses on Southern Boulevard, Chatham Township. The greenhouses were built in 1889 by Lord and Burnham. *Courtesy of Historical Society of the Township of Chatham*

Aerial view of Totty and Twombly greenhouses between Ridgedale and Greenwood avenues, Madison. *Courtesy of Madison Public Library*

The Swiss Knitting Mill was one of several mills that operated in Dover during its heyday as an industrial center for Morris County. The mill opened in 1896, manufacturing ladies and infants underwear. Photo circa 1910. *Courtesy of Lake Hopatcong Historical Society*

Jaqui's flour mills and residence, Morris Plains, circa 1895. *Courtesy of Morristown/Morris Township Free Public Library*

Boonton silk mill, circa 1905. *Courtesy of Boonton Historical Society and Museum*

Interior of Boonton silk mill, circa 1907. *Courtesy of Boonton Historical Society and Museum*

Construction of the Clyde Potts reservoir, Brookside, early 1900s. *Courtesy of Morristown/Morris Township Free Public Library*

Canal boat at the lumber yard near the Savage Road Bridge, Denville, 1896. *Courtesy of Denville Historical Society and Museum*

The Morris Canal went through the middle of Dover and then eastward on today's Route 46. This circa 1905 photograph shows the canal coming into Dover from Wharton parallel to today's Princeton Avenue. *Courtesy of Lake Hopatcong Historical Society*

The Morris Canal was a major reason for Lake Hopatcong's development. Stretching across northern New Jersey, the canal connected the Delaware and Hudson rivers until it was abandoned in 1924. Lake Hopatcong was its largest single source of water. Here a steamboat enters the outer lock at the current site of Hopatcong State Park, circa 1908. *Courtesy of Lake Hopatcong Historical Society*

The canal opened in the 1831, well before the invention of engine driven vehicles to bring coal east to Morris County iron makers. Canal boats were pulled by mules or horses in a journey of approximately 102 miles from end to end, taking three to five days to complete. *Courtesy Denville Historical Society*

Stanley mill, circa 1890. *Courtesy of Chatham Borough Historical Society*

A bird's eye view of the paper mill in Stanley, 1870. *Courtesy of Chatham Borough Historical Society*

The Bassett Dairy in Mine Hill, circa 1900. *Courtesy of Ferromonte Historical Society of Mine Hill*

Wharton Furnace, circa 1903. *Courtesy of Morris County Historical Society*

Hurd Mine in Wharton, circa 1905. Much of Morris County's early industry centered around iron mining. The county had rich veins of iron running through towns such as Mine Hill, Roxbury and Jefferson. Iron mining disappeared from Morris County when cheaper sources of iron were found in other parts of the country.
Courtesy of Lake Hopatcong Historical Society

Silk mill in Wharton, circa 1905. *Courtesy of Morris County Historical Society*

PUBLIC SERVICE

They look like the young men of today, and when they went to the Spanish-American War in 1898 they left amid a throng of cheering citizens in Dover. It was the same in Morristown years later when young soldiers shipped off to World War I, some leaning out train windows to say their last good-byes and shake hands. Crowds at both departures wore grim expressions, not a smile among them.

Earlier photos show Morris County soldiers who set off to fight the South in the Civil War. When Lincoln called for 75,000 militia on April 15, 1861, Joseph W. Revere of Morristown, grandson of Paul Revere, was the first New Jerseyan to volunteer for service. And when the flag was raised on the Green in Morristown the next day, most the town was there in a patriotic fever.

In more peaceful times, public service at the turn of the century often meant the same as it does now. Many men, nearly all of them mustachioed, served on fire companies. They fought with horse-drawn wagons and hook-and-ladder trucks and marched in parades with huge helmets and flat hats proclaiming their company ties. In time, the horses were replaced by fire engines and the mustaches disappeared.

Public service also meant serving in the Parsippany Police Department, such as the 10 men pictured from 1932. (There are more than 100 now.) Or it meant serving in government similar to the 25 officials — all older men in heavy dark suits — pictured in the Morris County Courthouse, spittoons waiting at their feet. At least that has changed.

Madison Fire Department hose wagon, circa 1895. The fireman on the wagon is Patrick Dougherty. *Courtesy of Madison Historical Society*

Resolute Hook and Ladder Company, Morristown Fire Department, circa 1890. *Courtesy of Morristown/Morris Township Free Public Library*

Resolute Hook and Ladder Company's horse-drawn wagon, circa 1885.
Courtesy of Morristown/Morris Township Free Public Library

Independent Hose Company, 2nd Carriage, Morristown Fire Department, circa 1890. *Courtesy of Morristown/Morris Township Free Public Library*

Special Committee of Independent Hose Company No. 1, Morristown Fire Department, circa 1900. Top row, J. Frank Lindsley, James R. Voorhees, Charles A. Covert, Henry M. Smith and Dr. Joseph R. Hoffman. Bottom row, Harrie T. Hull and Heyward G. Emmell. *Courtesy of Morristown/Morris Township Free Public Library*

Members of the Madison Fire Department with their new horse-drawn hose wagon, circa 1890. *Courtesy of Madison Historical Society*

Demonstration by the Morristown Fire Department. *Courtesy of Morristown/Morris Township Free Public Library*

The old Madison Hook & Ladder Co. before Hose Co. was formed. *Courtesy of Morristown/Morris Township Free Public Library*

Demonstration by the Morristown Fire Department. *Courtesy of Morristown/Morris Township Free Public Library*

Members of the Independent Hose Company, Morristown Fire Department, on the 25th anniversary of the company, 1888. Included in the photo are Augs. W. Bell, D.H. Rodney, Chas. H. Dalrymple, W.N. Corriell, F. E. Babitt, H.G. Wolff, Eugene Carrell, Dr. A.A. Lewis, J.F. Runyon, Chas. H. Green, G.E. Voorhees Jr., D.F. Sturges, J.F. Lindsley, J.R. Voorhees, H.B. Hoffman, J. B. Stevens, Frank Schuremand, Jas. McGuinnis, Jas. T. Clark, L.F. Sturges, Theo. Ayres, H.M. Smith, H.T. Hull, C.W. Ennis, C.S. Bird, Geo. C. Smith, W.H. Becker, I.R. Pierson, Dr. Jos. R. Hoffman, Geo. V. Muchmore, H. G. Emmell and E. Van Fleet. *Courtesy of Morristown/Morris Township Free Public Library*

Members of the Madison Fire Department in the early 1900s. *Courtesy of Madison Historical Society*

Boonton Fire Department hook and ladder truck during a Labor Day parade in 1915. *Courtesy of Morristown/Morris Township Free Public Library*

Banquet for the Mt. Tabor Fire Department, 1924. Clockwise from left, William Leighton, unidentified, Alex McClellan, Percy Quackenbush, William Walker, Robert Cantrell, William H., Lewis Glysencamp, Stephen Sofield, Harry Shaffer, Kenneth Gerard, William Glysencamp, Harold Baker, Claude Dickerson, unidentified, Raymond Parke Sr., unidentified, Elmer Dickerson, William Hill, unidentified, George Matthews, Winfield Vanderhoof, Albert Glysencamp, unidentified, Fred Lynch, Harvey Glysencamp, Lewis Dickerson, Elbert Fisher, Herman Kerscheim, William Wythe, Byram Moore, Harry Goble and George Earl. *Courtesy of Denville Historical Society and Museum*

Morristown Fire Department Engine Company No. 2, 1925. *Courtesy of Morristown/Morris Township Free Public Library*

Chief John J. Cullianan and his new car, Morristown, October 12, 1926. *Courtesy of Morristown/Morris Township Free Public Library*

A fire truck and some members of the Parsippany Fire Department in front of Lake Hiawatha Rotary Clubhouse, circa 1930. *Courtesy of Parsippany Historical and Preservation Society*

Green Village Volunteer Fire Department, Chatham Township, May 12, 1928. *Courtesy of Historical Society of the Township of Chatham*

Denville Fire Department inspection, October 7, 1939. Standing left to right, Peter Peer, William Keefe Sr., Stanley Peer, Russell Lash, Bill Green, William Champion, Bob Ronan, Ben Kinsley, Horace Cook, George Scott, Fred Jagger, Sam Vanorden, William Keefe Jr. and Carl Pascal. Middle row, Claude Mooney, William Jaggers, Ed Kible, Ben Dodson, John Dodson, Homer Peer, Lewis Peer, George VanOrden, Dan Peer, Charlie Salley and Burl Cook. Sitting, Claude Lash, Al Vialard, Fred Heider, Jim Lash, Howard Lash, George Keefe, Bob Lash, Adolph Forester, Ed Doremus, Karl Forester, Art Hopler Sr., Adelbert Doremus and Floyd Peer. *Courtesy of Denville Historical Society and Museum*

Madison Fire Department, circa 1935. *Courtesy of Madison Historical Society*

D.M. Merchant, first assistant chief of Morris Plains Fire Department, and veteran Morris Plains fireman John Cronshey stand behind the department's original hand pumper used in 1908. Photo taken prior to a parade in 1932. *Courtesy of Morris Plains Museum*

The Morris Plains Fire Department's new Waterous fire truck, purchased in 1923. The town had purchased its first mechanized apparatus, a Howe pumper on a Model T car chassis, in 1917. Unfortunately, the Howe was sitting in a boxcar waiting to be uncrated when fire destroyed half the business section in 1917. *Courtesy of Morris Plains Museum*

Madison Police Department, June 4, 1935. Front row: Anthony Giordano, Peter J. Farrell, Edward W. Hinch. Back row: Leon Doty, William T. Ryan, Orrin H. Atchison, Jim Ryan, John Walsh, William Kiernan and Martin P. Jennings. *Courtesy of Madison Public Library*

Members of the Madison Police Department in in front of the old Madison House, 1899. Those identified include Chief of Police Fred Johnson, John McGrath and Tom Radigau. *Courtesy of Morristown/Morris Township Free Public Library*

The Parsippany Police Department, circa 1930. *Courtesy of Parsippany Historical and Preservation Society*

Government officials at the Morris County Courthouse, circa 1900. *Courtesy of Morristown/Morris Township Free Public Library*

Morris Plains Mayor and Council, 1927. From left to right, front row, L.S. Young, Margaret Stang, Mayor D. M. Merchant, H. G. Vorburger, and Edward Connely. Back row, E. N. Babington, James Fear, Frank Millen, L. H. Burch, John Yawger, and Atty. David Barkman. *Courtesy of Morris County Historical Society*

Morris County Courthouse, Morristown, circa 1910. *Courtesy of Morristown/Morris Township Free Public Library*

Morris Plains Post Office on the first day of home delivery, 1936. Standing in front of the post office, from left to right, Frank Byrnes, Dr. R. V. D. Totten, Fred McGrath, James McErlane, Walter Coss, William Gilligan, Mayor Louis Burch and Dan Merchant. *Courtesy of Morris Plains Museum*

Members of the Hanover Township Committee, early 1900s. Many of these men later held elective office in the government of Parsippany-Troy Hills Township after it separated from Hanover in 1928. From left, front row, Ed Connelly, Harry Mead and Dr. Totten. Back row, Will Polhemus, Judd Condit, Will Davis, E. Halsey Ball and Will Webb. *Courtesy of Parsippany Historical and Preservation Society*

John Henry Hall, Company C - 7th Regiment, New Jersey Volunteer Infantry, on his return from Appomattox Courthouse, Virginia, after General Robert E. Lee's surrender in 1865. Hall, born in Denville, was 17 at the time of the photo.
Courtesy of Denville Historical Society and Museum

Private William Van Fleet (1836-1864). Van Fleet left his wife, Anna Doremus, and three small daughters to enlist in Company H (later Company K) of the New Jersey Volunteers. He died at Spotsylvania Court House, Virginia, May 12, 1864. *Courtesy of Parsippany Historical and Preservation Society*

Manning Blanchard of Denville in his Civil War uniform. Manning was born in 1833 at Beach Glen and died in 1910. *Courtesy of Denville Historical Society and Museum*

A crowd gathers in Dover to see Company M march by, circa 1898. *Courtesy of Morris County Historical Society*

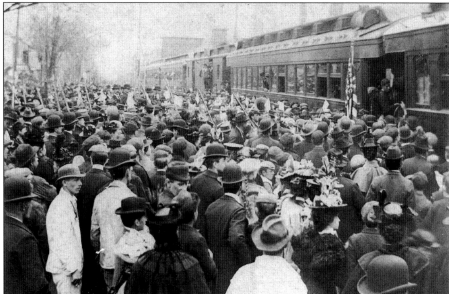

Company M boards the train in Dover for the Spanish American War, 1898. *Courtesy of Morris County Historical Society*

Crowds pack the streets of Dover to see off Company M for the Spanish American War, 1898. *Courtesy of Morris County Historical Society*

Company M marches in the streets of Dover as it prepares to go to the Spanish American War, circa 1898. *Courtesy of Morris County Historical Society*

Troops leaving Morristown during World War I. *Courtesy of Morristown/Morris Township Free Public Library*

Denville Home Guard, World War I. Standing left to right, Wallace Peer, Howard Baxter, William Clark, Arthur Peer, Russell Metz, George Lash and Harry Dickerson. Kneeling, George Freeman, Stewart Peer, Hugh Sweeney and Peter Peer. *Courtesy of Denville Historical Society and Museum*

The area we know as Picatinny Arsenal, located in Rockaway Township just north of Dover, has been interwoven with America's military since the Revolutionary War. From the forge that supplied George Washington's army to today's armaments research and development center, Picatinny played a major role in both World Wars, Korea and Vietnam. This is a view of the naval commander's home, circa 1930. *Courtesy of Picatinny Arsenal*

Early view of the administration building for the Naval Depot, built in 1902 at Picatinny Arsenal. *Courtesy of Picatinny Arsenal*

TRANSPORTATION

The automobile was the rising star back then, prize of the wealthy, a snooty interloper on roads that were neither made for them nor expected them.

The waning star was the steam engine, the iron behemoths that linked Morristown to New York in the east and Pennsylvania in the west. The two forms of transportation met shortly after the turn of the century, the start of something and the end of something.

The men and women in the first automobiles sat proudly, and stiffly, as if afraid the things could get away from them. Engineers and conductors (looking pretty much the same as they do now) stood equally proud in front of their steam engines on the Lackawanna Railroad. It's clear that both machines were the object of love.

There were other modes of transportation. The horse-drawn carriage was king then (the "stage wagon" began running between Jersey City and Morristown in 1771), but it was on the way out. The automobile, although in its infancy, was already having accidents, as evidenced by the photograph of an overturned car in Morristown.

Steamers like the Hopatcong plied the state's largest lake. The trolley made it to Dover and Boonton and got frozen in its tracks in big snowstorms.

The 102-mile Morris Canal between the Hudson and the Delaware, which brought coal east to the fuel-starved forges in Morris County, began losing out to the train almost as soon as it opened in 1831. Only seven years later the railroad reached Morristown.

Louis A. Noe in his new Buick, Chatham Township, circa 1915. *Courtesy of Historical Society of the Township of Chatham*

Second locomotive "Madison #24" built in 1880. The number was changed to 445 in 1889. The locomotive was scrapped in 1907. Note the Statue of Liberty on the lantern, Madison, circa 1886. *Courtesy of Madison Public Library*

Convent Station, located near St. Elizabeth's Convent, circa 1885. *Courtesy of Morristown/Morris Township Free Public Library*

Chatham railroad station, circa 1890. *Courtesy of Morristown/Morris Township Free Public Library*

The Morristown train station, February 1898. *Courtesy of Morristown/Morris Township Free Public Library*

This unissued stock certificate dates from 1895, when the creation of the Whippany River Railroad (WRRR) enabled the many paper mills in and around Whippany to grow and prosper. Construction on the 4-mile railroad began on April 22, 1895 and ran along a twisting route to Morristown where it connected with the Delaware, Lackawanna & Western Railroad. By August 16th of the same year, the WRRR was operating its first freight train. The line however, was very poorly built, and by November 1895 the company was bankrupt due to its inability to pay off its construction loans. *Courtesy of Steven Hepler Collection*

The Madison, NJ station of the Delaware, Lackawanna & Western Railroad (DL&W) was opened to the public on April 17, 1916. The Collegiate Gothic-style depot features this interior staircase that leads to the eastbound (Hoboken) tracks. *Courtesy of Whippany Railway Museum*

The diminutive locomotive, Morristown & Erie R.R. (M&E) No. 2, circa 1911. Built in 1894 by the American Locomotive Company's Rhode Island Works for the Chicago Southside Elevated R.R., this unusual "Forney"-type locomotive was acquired by the M&E in February 1908 and was placed into local passenger service between Morristown, Whippany and Essex Fells, NJ. Loved by passengers and crew alike, No. 2 was alternately nicknamed "The Dinky" and "The Peanut Roaster." In 1922 she was sold to the Hanover Brick Company in Whippany, where the engine worked until the plant closed in 1931. Afterwards, a forlorn looking No. 2 sat on the M&E's coal dock at Morristown for five years until she was scrapped in 1936. *Courtesy of Whippany Railway Museum*

The gatehouse at Fox Hill where Martha Ann (Husk) Mattoon was gate tender for the Delaware, Lakawanna and Western Railroad. She was the first woman to hold such a position. Included in the photo are Mattoon's daughters, Hannah Mattoon and Lily Rogers. The man is a railroad track worker. *Courtesy of Denville Historical Society and Museum*

Engine No. 1, Morristown, late 1800s. *Courtesy of Morristown/Morris Township Free Public Library*

Morristown railroad station, circa 1900. *Courtesy of Morristown/Morris Township Free Public Library*

Railroad employees, from left to right: Frank Hazelton, flagman, Joseph Freary, baggage master, Edward Bickel, conductor, George Hand, fireman, and Theodore Mills, engineer, Morristown, circa 1900. *Courtesy of Morristown/Morris Township Free Public Library*

Railroad employees. Top row, left to right: DeWitt McCathron, engineer, Hugh Williams, fireman. Bottom row: Kirk Webter, flagman, George Stevens, conductor, George Haas, baggage master, and Daniel Parks, brakeman, Morristown, circa 1900. *Courtesy of Morristown/Morris Township Free Public Library*

Albian Page in his early automobile, Chatham Township, circa 1905. *Courtesy of Historical Society of the Township of Chatham*

Wharton train station, circa 1900. *Courtesy of Morris County Historical Society*

Railroad Station, Mendham, circa 1905. *Courtesy of Morris County Historical Society*

Denville train tower before 1903. *Courtesy of Denville Historical Society and Museum*

Lackawanna Railroad entering Madison through James Park prior to elevation of railroad tracks. James Library and James Building are visible in the background, circa 1910. *Courtesy of Madison Public Library*

The Boonton Line trolley at Horton's Ice Cream Shop, Denville Station, circa 1914. *Courtesy of Denville Historical Society and Museum*

Nelson Cobb in his horse-drawn carriage, Denville, circa 1900. *Courtesy of Denville Historical Society and Museum*

A seven-passenger Packard Thirty, owned and driven by Jack Humbert, on Main Street, Madison, enroute to a Princeton-Yale game at Princeton, circa 1910. Also in the automobile are Curtis McGraw, Ted Humbert and James McGraw. Standing are Andy Gee and Fred Douglas. *Courtesy of Madison Public Library*

Delaware, Lakawanna and Western Railroad, Morristown train station, circa 1904. *Courtesy of Morristown/Morris Township Free Public Library*

Trolley in Madison in front of what was later the Penny Press, Park Avenue and Main Street intersection. Raymond Lyon was the conductor and Walter Raymond the motorman, 1912. *Courtesy of Madison Public Library*

The Morris County Traction Company introduced trolleys to northwestern New Jersey. At its peak, the company's service stretched from Newark and Elizabeth to Lake Hopatcong. This picture depicts the arrival of trolley service in Boonton, circa 1910. *Courtesy of Lake Hopatcong Historical Society*

Dover was the first town to receive trolley service from the Morris County Traction Company in 1904. This photo shows trolleys stranded during the winter of 1914 on Blackwell Street in Dover. *Courtesy of Lake Hopatcong Historical Society*

Visitors mill around the train station at Nolans Point, circa 1905. Tourism began to boom at Lake Hopatcong when the Central Railroad of New Jersey reached the lake in the early 1880s. *Courtesy of Lake Hopatcong Historical Society*

Lackawanna Railroad at Wharton with the Wharton Furnace on the right, circa 1900. *Courtesy of Lake Hopatcong Historical Society*

The White Line steamer Hopatcong, circa 1905. Steamboats serviced all areas of Lake Hopatcong. They had schedules with regular stops at the major hotels and designated docks. In addition, one could request steamboat pickup by placing a flag on any dock. *Courtesy of Lake Hopatcong Historical Society*

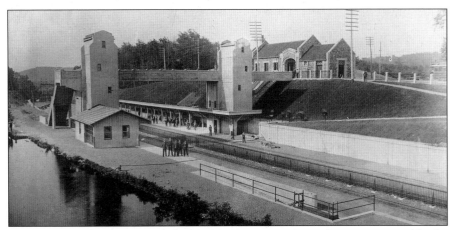

The Morris and Essex Railroad was the first railroad at Lake Hopatcong. Tracks were laid through Landing in the 1850s, but since there was no station, arriving passengers had to disembark at Drakesville (now Ledgewood). A station was finally built at Landing in the 1880s. Since the railroad and Morris Canal were side-by-side, arriving passengers could cross the platform and board a waiting steamboat, which would take them to their destination on Lake Hopatcong. The station at Landing was greatly modernized in 1910 as seen in this 1911 photograph. *Courtesy of Lake Hopatcong Historical Society*

Auto accident in Morristown, circa 1915. *Courtesy of Morristown/Morris Township Free Public Library*

Visitors pose with the crew of a Central Railroad of New Jersey excursion train to Lake Hopatcong at Nolans Point, circa 1900. *Courtesy of Lake Hopatcong Historical Society*

The Lackawanna Railroad station for Lake Hopatcong at Landing is on the right as a Morris County Traction Company trolley passes by, circa 1915. The train station building survives today, although it has been used for commercial purposes since the 1980s. *Courtesy of Lake Hopatcong Historical Society*

Vehicle from Dover parade commemorating the end of World War I in 1919. *Courtesy of Lake Hopatcong Historical Society*

Down's used car lot, Morristown, circa 1920. *Courtesy of Morristown/Morris Township Free Public Library*

Out for a drive in Morris County, circa 1920. *Courtesy of Morristown/Morris Township Free Public Library*

Early mode of transportation on Bank Street, Morristown, circa 1910. *Courtesy of Morristown/Morris Township Free Public Library*

Auto show at the Morris County Fair, September 1923. *Courtesy of Morristown/Morris Township Free Public Library*

Horace and Maggie Peer with their dog, Jack, in front of their new car, circa 1926. *Courtesy of Denville Historical Society and Museum*

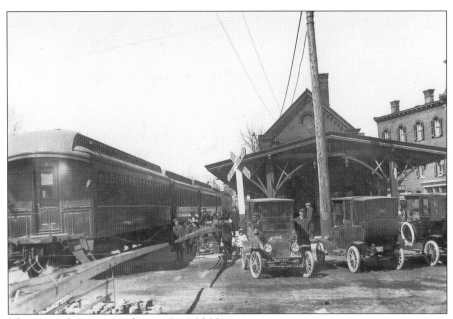

The train depot at Madison, circa 1910. *Courtesy of Madison Public Library*

Engine #946 pulls away from the Madison depot, circa 1910. *Courtesy of Madison Public Library*

RESIDENTIAL

Not everyone lived in big frame houses surrounded by picket fences, although you might think so from the following sampling of Morris County homes about 100 years ago.

True, Morristown and other towns had their share of the poor and ramshackle. Here, though, are some of the best houses. These were the ones people wanted to see. And photograph. Most are three-story. Some are gargantuan. All bespeak a kind of wealth and success and the quiet solitude that the fortunate still enjoy in Morris County.

You might recognize some of these homes, oddly formal and strangely silent in the cold stare of the camera. Others are gone for things like supermarket parking lots and the arrival of the hundreds of thousands of new people who in 100 years raised Morris County's population from 65,156 in 1900 to 470,212 in 2000.

One hundred years ago, there were no garages. No condos. No traffic lights. No big box stores. There were just big houses towering over little picket fences, no doubt to keep the horses out.

The Charles Dickerson House stood at the corner of Diamond Spring Road and Main Street, Denville, now the location of a Grand Union parking lot. The house was built in 1856 and torn down in 1956. *Courtesy of Denville Historical Society and Museum*

The George Bowlsby house on Baldwin Road off Route 46 in Parsippany. The house was built by Bowlsby circa 1790. It serves today as the Parsippany Historic Museum. *Courtesy of Parsippany Historical and Preservation Society*

The Tower House, Morris Township, home of William Ketchell, New Jersey state geologist. This home was occupied by the Roosevelt family for three summers between 1870-1875. It is believed that President Theodore Roosevelt is the young man on the pony. Photo circa late 1800s. *Courtesy of Morristown/Morris Township Free Public Library*

George Shephard Page and Lorenza Way in front of the Way residence on River Road, Stanley, 1884. *Courtesy of Chatham Borough Historical Society*

The Page house, built by George Shepard Page in 1867, Chatham Township. *Courtesy of Historical Society of the Township of Chatham*

Evans homestead on Casterline Road, Denville, circa 1900. *Courtesy of Denville Historical Society and Museum*

Charles Noble home in Morristown, circa 1900. *Courtesy of Morristown/Morris Township Free Public Library*

Early home on Brittin Street, Madison. *Courtesy of Morristown/Morris Township Free Public Library*

Residence of Mrs. Alexander Tiers, also know as Farmlands, on Sand Spring Road, Harding. *Courtesy of Morris County Historical Society*

Home on Ridgedale Avenue, Madison, late 1800s. *Courtesy of Madison Historical Society*

"Crown Hill" on Green Avenue, Madison, was the home of Jacob S. Paulmier. *Courtesy of Madison Historical Society*

James C. Holden house at 73 Prospect Street, Madison, was built about 1870 by James C. Holden, Madison. *Courtesy of Madison Public Library*

Seaman mansion on Union Hill, Madison, circa 1913, was demolished when the elevated railroad was put in. *Courtesy of Madison Public Library*

James A. Webb house on Kings and Green Village roads, Madison, was called the "Home on the Bank." *Courtesy of Madison Public Library*

The Lake Hopatcong "cottage" of Woodbury, N.J., "patent medicine" king Col. George G. Green, circa 1915. Green built this home in the Mount Harry section of Mount Arlington in 1890. *Courtesy of Lake Hopatcong Historical Society*

The Bassett homestead on Randolph Avenue, Mine Hill, circa 1900. Richard Bassett Sr. stands on the right. Richard Bassett Jr. stands behind him, next to the house. Richard Bassett Jr. served as the Randolph tax collector in addition to working for his family's dairy and delivering milk to customers in Randolph, Mine Hill, Kenvil, Wharton and Dover. *Courtesy of Morris County Historical Society*

The Ford Mansion, Washington's headquarters during the Revolutionary War, Morristown. *Courtesy of Morristown/Morris Township Free Public Library*

Ira Lindsley home on Madison Avenue, Morris Township, 1892. *Courtesy of Morristown/Morris Township Free Public Library*

Residence of Dr. H. Raymond and Dr. Julia C. Mutchler on West Blackwell Street, Dover, circa 1935. *Courtesy of Morris County Historical Society*

Residence of H.C. Jenkins, Boonton, circa 1900. *Courtesy of Morristown/Morris Township Free Public Library*

Mr. & Mrs. Frederick H. Clarke with their dog, Mike, in front of the home of Homer Davenport on Tabor Road, Morris Plains, 1909. *Courtesy of Morristown/Morris Township Free Public Library*

RECREATION

People were so innocent and so naïve-looking then. Posing with the basketball team (or baseball team, or football team) they looked so... well... clean. The hair was coifed, uniforms were primitively simple. On the tennis court they wore long skirts, ties and straw boaters. They did not wear football helmets or tennis shoes. They were gentle men and gentle women, and although they loved their sports, they kept them in perspective, except for baseball. Baseball was big then. Towns had teams, and sometimes teams had towns.

Baseball wasn't the only way to while away the time. They went to the circus (which came by train, not truck). They went to Lake Hopatcong and rode the roller coaster at Bertand Island and spent 25 cents for a swim at Lee's Park. They camped. And fished. They watched now-funny-looking cars race along dirt roads. And picnicked.

The richer folk frequented the horse clubs or the golf clubs. In short, they did many of the same things then that we do now, but at a more leisurely pace.

Boonton YMCA basketball team of 1914-1915. Left to right, Y. Pennington, Walter Morton, Barry Dawson, Sam Basch, unidentified, Tom Dennison and Marcus Barsch. *Courtesy of Boonton Historical Society and Museum*

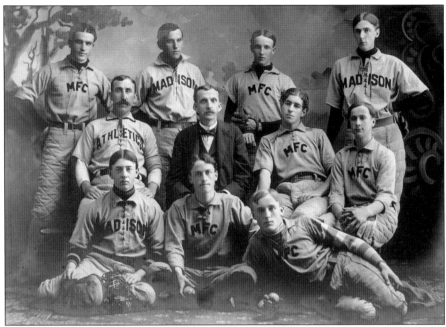

Madison Field Club of 1899. Back row, from left, Harry Card, 2nd base; John Suling, shortstop; Robert Troxell, center field; Robert Paulmier, 3rd base. Middle row, J. B. McGrath, 1st base, captain; Fred B. Bardon, manager; Floyd Lanning, right field; Vernon Lum, left field. Front row, William Keane, catcher; Charles Hamilton, pitcher; C. W. Vreeland, pitcher. *Courtesy of Madison Public Library*

Parlor games in 1897. From left, front row, Hannah Thompson, Daisy Mathis and Estelle Turquand. Back row, Margaret Rogers, Alinda Reeves and Alice Hazelton. *Courtesy of Parsippany Historical and Preservation Society*

Members of the Silver Star Tennis Club, Morristown, circa 1888. *Courtesy of Morristown/Morris Township Free Public Library*

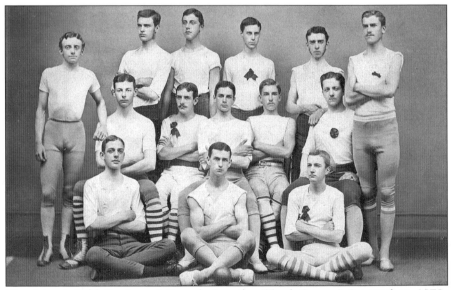

Morristown Athletic Association during the "Track-Games," September, 1878. Those listed are: Willard Walker Outler, Mahlon Pitney III, Walter B. Wood, Theo. Ayers Jr., Carman Fitz-Randolph, Frederick Winston Merrell, Henry Springler, Von Erden Davis, Paul Revere, William Meeker Wood, Henry C. Pitney Jr., John O.H. Pitney, Thomas M. Fitz, Robert Wrightson Webb. *Courtesy of Morristown/Morris Township Free Public Library*

Baseball team, Hazen School, Morristown, 1904. *Courtesy of Morristown/Morris Township Free Public Library*

Circus unloading at the railroad depot, Morristown, early 1900s. *Courtesy of Morristown/Morris Township Free Public Library*

Boonton's first football team, 1893. From left, top row, E. Blanchard, H. Conn, R. Dawson, F. Pennington. Middle row, J. Oliver, J. Culvert, N. Dawson, H. Culvert and W. Collins. Front row, J. Myers, G. Bird, F. Barker and Shorty Bates. *Courtesy of Boonton Historical Society and Museum*

Tennis Club, Olyphant Park, Morristown, late 1800s. *Courtesy of Morristown/Morris Township Free Public Library*

Members of the horse club, early 1900s. *Courtesy of Morristown/Morris Township Free Public Library*

Morris County Golf Club, circa 1900. *Courtesy of Chatham Borough Historical Society*

Spectators watch the auto races, Morris County, early 1900s. *Courtesy of Morristown/Morris Township Free Public Library*

Auto racing in Morris County, early 1900s. *Courtesy of Morristown/Morris Township Free Public Library*

Florham Park baseball team, 1905. *Courtesy of Madison Historical Society*

Fishing on Shongum Lake, Randolph, circa 1900. *Courtesy of Historical Society of the Township of Chatham*

The Boonton Jerseys baseball team of 1905. From left, front row, John Conn, Mickey Quick, Eddie Shanahan, Joe McCormick, John Bolster, Frank Richards and Bill Lucas. Back row, Ernie Scribner, Pat Cooney, Jim Carey, Jesse Voorhees, Eddie Kotcher, Jim Hopler, Alec Lewis, Ed Burgess and Bill Lewis. *Courtesy of Boonton Historical Society and Museum*

Jersey Field Club of Boonton, circa 1906. *Courtesy of Boonton Historical Society and Museum*

This team, popularly known as "The Victors," was a favorite with Boonton fans in the early 1900s. They played at West Boonton Ball Park. From left, front row, Frank Emerick, William Maher, Walter Emerick, John Gregory and William Estler. Back row, Daniel Carey, William Reilly, James Sullivan, James Benjamin, Martin Bickler and Edward Short. *Courtesy of Boonton Historical Society and Museum*

Morristown High School basketball team. First row, left to right: Merritt Ambrose, Harry Couch, Ray Leggiett, Orville Meslar, Ashton Davis, Richard Horsefield, unidentified. Second row: Joseph DeBrott, Harry Davis, Edward Vaughan, Henry Williamson, William Carr, Judson Vaughan. Third row: George Goeke, Elwood Holley, early 1900s. *Courtesy of Morristown/Morris Township Free Public Library*

Louis A. Noe with his 1913 Noe Farm baseball team on Southern Boulevard, Chatham Township. *Courtesy of Historical Society of the Township of Chatham*

Jack Dempsey, heavy-weight champion of the world, 1919-1926, trained at the Welsh Health Farm, Chatham Township. *Courtesy of Historical Society of the Township of Chatham*

Freddie Welsh, lightweight champion of the world, 1914-1917. After retiring in 1922, Welsh bought a health farm in Chatham Township where boxers such as Jack Dempsey came to train. *Courtesy of Historical Society of the Township of Chatham*

Boxing training at Madame Boys, Chatham Township. *Courtesy of Historical Society of the Township of Chatham*

George Hessey's Band, Boonton, circa 1917. From left, back row, George Hessey, John Gonda, John Rak, Pete Barna, John Mraz, Jack Kostka, John Kufta and Walter Gonda. Front row, Steve Chuey, Pete Marcello, Dick Richards, Andrew Kominiak and Martin Hornik. *Courtesy of Boonton Historical Society and Museum*

Hillside Field Club of Boonton, 1911. From left, front row, Mehalik, Downey, Sikora, Fowler and Norrie. Back row, Dennison, Maraz, McCormick, Lucas, Norrie and Basch. *Courtesy of Boonton Historical Society and Museum*

Jersey Field Club of Boonton, 1912. *Courtesy of Boonton Historical Society and Museum*

Dover YMCA baseball team of 1913. From left, E. Paeker, E. Cooper, W. Hopkins, R. May, J. Casterline, T. Dennison, H. Pedrick, S. Pedrick, J. Pedrick, P. Pierce and E. Maloney.
Courtesy of Boonton Historical Society and Museum

The YMCA building on Main Street, Madison. *Courtesy of Madison Public Library*

Fishing has always been a favorite attraction for visitors to Lake Hopatcong. Only catfish, sunfish and yellow perch are considered native to the lake, circa 1910.
Courtesy of Lake Hopatcong Historical Society

Steamer Uncle Dan arriving at Hotel Breslin, Lake Hopatcong, circa 1910. Since roads at the lake were poor or nonexistent, the main source of transportation during Lake Hopatcong's early years was by water. As tourism developed, so did steamboat service. The Lake Hopatcong Steamboat Company, commonly known as the Black Line, was founded in 1886 and provided service from the railroads to all areas of the lake. In 1890, a competing steamboat company was founded and they engaged in lively competition through the teens. *Courtesy of Lake Hopatcong Historical Society*

The beach at Bertrand Island, circa 1908. Morris County Traction Company extended trolley service to the beach in 1910, and amusements soon followed. The beach would evolve into Bertrand Island Amusement Park. *Courtesy of Lake Hopatcong Historical Society*

The Lake Hopatcong Yacht Club was founded in 1905 and broke ground for its clubhouse on Bertrand Island in 1909. This 1910 photograph was taken just after the dedication of the clubhouse. *Courtesy of Lake Hopatcong Historical Society*

While most working people in the late 19th century could not afford more than a day at a resort such as Lake Hopatcong, there was a developing middle class that was beginning to have the time and money for leisure activities and vacations. Camping was a popular and cheaper alternative to hotels, as seen by this photo of a camp in the King Cove (Landing) section of Lake Hopatcong, circa 1910. *Courtesy of Lake Hopatcong Historical Society*

Bertrand Island Amusement Park, circa 1930. The park was a landmark at Lake Hopatcong from the early 1900s until it closed in 1983. It was a favorite destination for generations of school and church outings, as well as company picnics. *Courtesy of Lake Hopatcong Historical Society*

The construction of a roller coaster in 1925 transformed Bertrand Island into a full amusement park. Over the years, the park featured some 20 rides, a boardwalk full of games, a dance hall, picnic pavilion, sand beach and more. *Courtesy of Lake Hopatcong Historical Society*

Sightseeing boats were a popular feature throughout Bertrand Island Amusement Park's existence, as seen in this circa 1930s photograph. *Courtesy of Lake Hopatcong Historical Society*

Seen here just after opening, the June Rose Ballroom was built at Bertrand Island in 1923. In the 1920s and 1930s, it was a popular place to dance to the sound of big bands. It was renamed Bertrand Island Villa in 1949. *Courtesy of Lake Hopatcong Historical Society*

Bertrand Island's first Ferris wheel arrived in 1930 and quickly became a favorite way to view the lake. *Courtesy of Lake Hopatcong Historical Society*

Lee's Park was one of numerous private beaches that operated at Lake Hopatcong during the lake's great resort years. In the 1990s it was donated by the Lee family to Morris County and is now operated as a county marina. Photo circa 1930. *Courtesy of Lake Hopatcong Historical Society*

Camping offered the cheapest option for a vacation. All that was needed was a piece of ground and a tent. Many individuals rented land and pitched a tent for a week or more at a time. Some camps would even rent you the tent, as seen in this circa 1910 photograph of Camp Village in the Prospect Point (Jefferson) section of Lake Hopatcong. *Courtesy of Lake Hopatcong Historical Society*

Advertisement for the Palace Theatre in Netcong, circa 1939. Originally opened as a vaudeville theater, the Palace evolved to movies. During Hollywood's heyday of the 1930s, the Palace, like many theaters nationwide, changed movies three times per week. *Courtesy of Lake Hopatcong Historical Society*

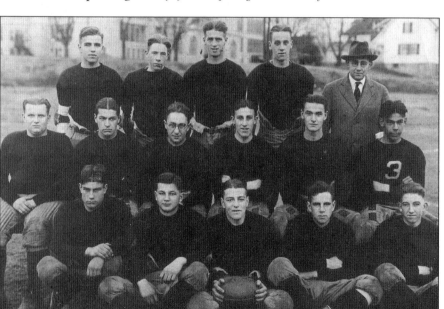

Morristown High School football team, 1923. *Courtesy of Morristown/Morris Township Free Public Library*

Morristown High School girls basketball team, 1928. *Courtesy of Morristown/Morris Township Free Public Library*

Burnham Park, Morristown, 1920s. *Courtesy of Morristown/Morris Township Free Public Library*

Madison Academy baseball team, 1928. *Courtesy of Madison Public Library*

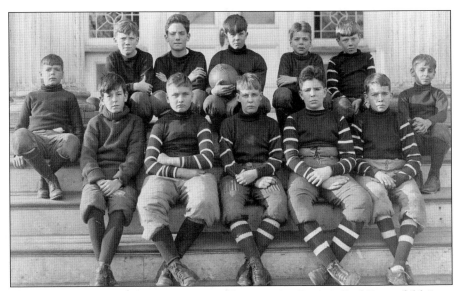

Madison Academy football team, 1922. Top row, Art Rogers, Rod Rosenfeld, Lew Rosenfeld, Bob Palmer, Andy Rogers, William Ludlow and Bill Sterns. Bottom row, Ralph Johnson, George Buckingham, Charles Decker, Lane Lovell and John Harrison. *Courtesy of Madison Historical Society*

The Lake Hiawatha Clubhouse at the southwest corner of North Beverwyck Road and Minnehaha, circa 1930. *Courtesy of Parsippany Historical and Preservation Society*

Summer cabin at Lake Hiawatha, Troy Hills, circa 1930. *Courtesy of Parsippany Historical and Preservation Society*

SOCIETY

It's hard to imagine women not having the right to vote. Or suffragists marching (or driving open-air cars and taking their campaign to boats on Lake Hopatcong) for the 19th Amendment to the Constitution. Their campaign was part of society back then, and their battle needed to be won.

The churches our ancestors built were big, imposing, often beautiful structures, and in this new century many remain, joined by others, although their roles in our lives have changed. Presbyterian. Baptist. Episcopal. Methodist. You can see them all today in a walk though Morristown. Perhaps no other buildings in town look as much the same now as they did then.

We were joiners. There was the Morristown Club. The Whippany River Club. The Golf Club. The Rotary Club. The Fife and Drum Corps of Troy Hills. And the Pocahontas Lodge of the Red Woman.

Things are so different today. And so much the same. For some things, only the names have changed, and for the Rotary Club not even that.

Members of the Pocahontas Lodge of the Red Woman, Morristown, circa 1917. *Courtesy of Morristown/Morris Township Free Public Library*

Joseph Percy Crayon, 1841-1908. He was a Denville Civil War veteran and historian and published the book "Rockaway Records" in 1902, chronicling the genealogies of most families in the Denville/Rockaway area, circa 1868. *Courtesy of Denville Historical Society and Museum*

Hilltop Presbyterian Church on Mountain Avenue, Mendham. The church was built in 1860 after fire destroyed earlier edifices. *Courtesy of Morris County Historical Society*

Presbyterian Church, Morristown, circa 1870. *Courtesy of Morristown/Morris Township Free Public Library*

Construction of the Presbyterian Church, circa 1892. *Courtesy of Morristown/Morris Township Free Public Library*

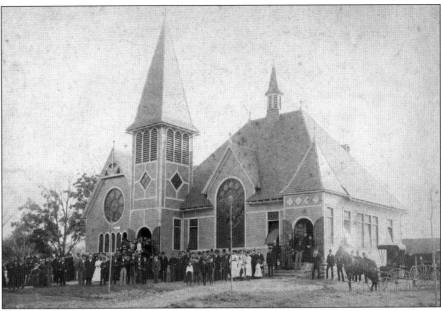

The congregation gathers in front of the Presbyterian church in Dover, circa 1890. The church was struck by lightning in 1899. *Courtesy of Morris County Historical Society*

The crowded parking area in front of the Presbyterian Church in Hanover, September 17, 1890. *Courtesy of Morris County Historical Society*

The Troy Hills Fife and Drum Corps, circa 1890. *Courtesy of Parsippany Historical and Preservation Society*

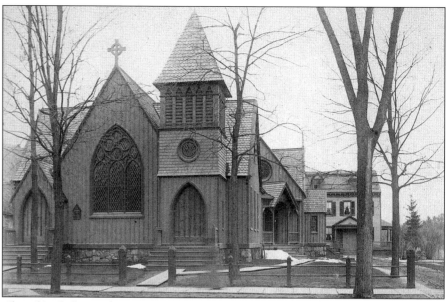

Church of the Redeemer on South Street, Morristown, June 1891. *Courtesy of Morristown/Morris Township Free Public Library*

First Baptist Church, built in 1893 at Washington Street and Cattano Avenue, Morristown, circa 1900. Gutted by arson in 2000, it is being rebuilt. *Courtesy of Morristown/Morris Township Free Public Library*

Methodist Church, Morristown, late 1800s. *Courtesy of Morristown/Morris Township Free Public Library*

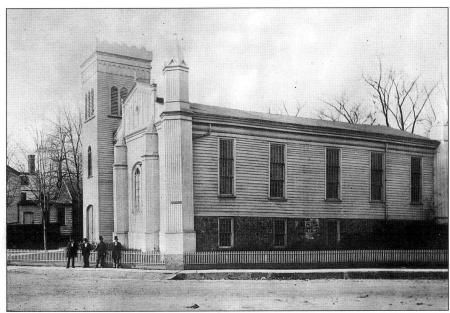

The old Baptist Church on Speedwell Avenue, Morristown, was erected in 1845, photo, circa 1900. *Courtesy of Morristown/Morris Township Free Public Library*

The Parsippany Methodist Church as seen from Route 46. Land was acquired in 1830, but lack of funding delayed the completion of the church until 1843. The building was demolished in the early 1960s. *Courtesy of Parsippany Historical and Preservation Society*

Interior of St. Peter's Episcopal church at Christmas, Morristown, 1905. *Courtesy of Morristown/Morris Township Free Public Library*

St. Virgil's Church at the southwest corner of West Hanover Avenue, Morris Plains, 1890. *Courtesy of Morris Plains Museum*

Dinner commemorating the 25th Anniversary of the organization of the Morristown Club, June 22, 1909. *Courtesy of Morristown/Morris Township Free Public Library*

Mendham Presbyterian Church, circa 1900. *Courtesy of Morristown/Morris Township Free Public Library*

Green Village Methodist Church men's class, Chatham Township, early 1900s. *Courtesy of Historical Society of the Township of Chatham*

Members of the Women's Suffrage movement, Morristown. *Courtesy of Morristown/Morris Township Free Public Library*

Women's Suffrage movement members, Morristown. *Courtesy of Morristown/Morris Township Free Public Library*

Automobile used by the Women's Suffrage group, driven by Miss Sarah Crowell. Passengers are Miss Ann Skinner, Mrs. Amelia Moorfield and Mrs. Sommer. *Courtesy of Morristown/Morris Township Free Public Library*

Suffragists campaigning on Lake Hopatcong, 1915. *Courtesy of Lake Hopatcong Historical Society*

Annual fall dinner of the North Jersey Society for the Promotion of Agriculture held at the Golf Club, Morristown, October 17, 1913. *Courtesy of Morristown/Morris Township Free Public Library*

St Peter's Episcopal Church, Morristown. *Courtesy of Morristown/Morris Township Free Public Library*

Presbyterian Church, Morristown, circa 1900. *Courtesy of Morristown/Morris Township Free Public Library*

Members of the Whippany River Club, circa 1910. *Courtesy of Morristown/Morris Township Free Public Library*

Members of the Rotary Club by Shelly's Ice House, Morristown. *Courtesy of Morristown/Morris Township Free Public Library*

Hurdtown Methodist
Church in Jefferson.
*Courtesy of Morris County
Historical Society*

Cast of a centennial
pageant gather in
front of the
Parsippany
Presbyterian
Church in June
1929. *Courtesy of Morris
County Historical Society*

Old Folks Concert at Parsippany Presbyterian Church. Those in the photo include; Edward Kimbald, Henry Grimes, Mildred Righter, Ed Ball, Mary Cooper, Andrew L. Cobb, Caroline Horvel, Henry Brown, unidentified, Estelle Young, Edna Righter, Mary Cobb, Gertrude Leonard, Dr. E.P. Cooper, Mrs. Cooper, Elizabeth Cobb, Grace Baldwin, Annie Brown, William Casper, unidentified, unidentified, Louise Young, Jackson Bates, Louis Cooper Craig and Judd Condit. *Courtesy of Morris County Historical Society*

Citizens Band of Madison. *Courtesy of Madison Historical Society*

CELEBRATION

Perhaps no parade will top the celebration at Dover's Old Home Carnival, a week-long civic and patriotic extravaganza in the heat of August 1910. There wasn't just one parade — there were four, one every day for four days in a row.

On the first day, after church services, there was a civic parade of businessmen and more than 50 merchants on horseback in uniforms and white duck trousers. Wagons and floats, more than 80 of them, made their way through crowds of thousands of well-dressed people beneath buildings with more bunting and flags than Morris County may ever have seen before or after. You would have thought it was the end of World War I, which was still years away.

The second day, following a 25-piece band and a young king and queen in a chariot, more than 240 babies were feted in a baby parade. (The one chosen the prettiest rode in a cart pulled by a St. Bernard.) The third day there was a parade of 30 automobiles — they were still new then. The fourth day's parade, of firemen, was the largest of all. (Rockaway and Wharton won first and second prize.) Fire companies still put on the biggest and longest parades in Morris County.

All decked out for the Old Home Week parade in Dover, 1910. *Courtesy of Morris County Historical Society*

The Old Home Week parade in Dover, 1910. *Courtesy of Morris County Historical Society*

Dover parade commemorating end of World War I and the return of the veterans. The parade, held in 1919, was led by a U.S. Army band. *Courtesy of Lake Hopatcong Historical Society*

Ready to roll for the Old Home Week parade in Dover, 1910. *Courtesy of Morris County Historical Society*

Parade down Main Street, Boonton, circa 1915. *Courtesy of Boonton Historical Society and Museum*

Dedication of the Fort Nonsense monument, Morristown, April 28, 1888. *Courtesy of Morristown/Morris Township Free Public Library*

Denville's George Washington Bicentennial celebration, August 1932. *Courtesy of Denville Historical Society and Museum*

Dover parade commemorating the end of World War I. *Courtesy of Picatinny Arsenal*

Dover Fire Department marches down West Blackwell Street in Dover during the Old Home Week celebration, 1910. *Courtesy of Morris County Historical Society*